SUSTAINING OUR ENVIRONMENT

Waste and Pollution

Rufus Bellamy

FRANKLIN WATTS
LONDON • SYDNEY

First published in 2009 by
Franklin Watts
338 Euston Road
London NW1 3BH

Franklin Watts Australia
Level 17/207 Kent Street
Sydney NSW 2000

Series editor: Adrian Cole
Art director: Jonathan Hair
Design: Simon Borrough
Picture research: Diana Morris

Acknowledgements:

*Special thanks to Christian Aid for their help with this title and for permission
to include the story of the Forgotten Poor on page 14.*

G.M.B. Akash/Panos: 14, 37. Wes Allison/Honda: 32. Chris Martin Bahr/Rex Features: 18. Santosh
Bane/Greenpeace: 27. Natalie Behring/Panos: 26. Daniel Betrå/ Greenpeace: 13. Stéphane
Bidouzec/Shutterstock: 8. Ben Blackenburg/istockphoto: 10. Blacksmith Institute: 24. DIY
Photolibrary/Construction Photography: 22. Envirofit.org: 31t, 31c. Graham Flack/Recycle Now
Partners: 19. Martin Harvey/Gallo/Getty Images: 41. Mark Henley/Panos: 21. Paul Lowe/Panos: 9.
Gerd Ludwig/Panos: 11. Mikkel Ostergaard/Panos: front cover. Jim Parkin/istockphoto: 33.
Playpumps.org: 36. prism68/Shutterstock: 16. Recycle Now Partners: 16b, 17. Lajos Repasi/
istockphoto: 40. Jiri Rezac/Greenpeace: 20. David Rose/Panos: 25. Sengkang: 15c, 15b. Andreas
Schoelzel/Greenpeace: 29. Sipa Press/Rex Features: 35. Sean Sprague/Panos: 30 Sydney Water: 38.
Tlady7/istockphoto: 23b. Sven Torfinn/Panos: 39. Jim West/Alamy: 28. Tom Wood/Alamy: 34.

Every attempt has been made to clear copyright. Should there be any inadvertent omission
please apply to the publisher for rectification.

A CIP catalogue record for this book is available from the British Library.

Dewey number: 363.72'8

ISBN: 978 0 7496 8827 1

Printed in China

Franklin Watts is a division of Hachette Children's Books, an Hachette UK company.
www.hachette.co.uk

Contents

The waste and pollution challenge

Pollution takes many forms, from car emissions, to untreated waste from a pig farm. It contaminates and harms the environment and can affect the health of living things, reducing their quality of life. Pollution can kill people, plants and animals and has been highlighted as a key cause for the loss of biodiversity around the world.

▼ When we throw away waste we aren't just creating pollution and causing a mess like this, we are also wasting resources.

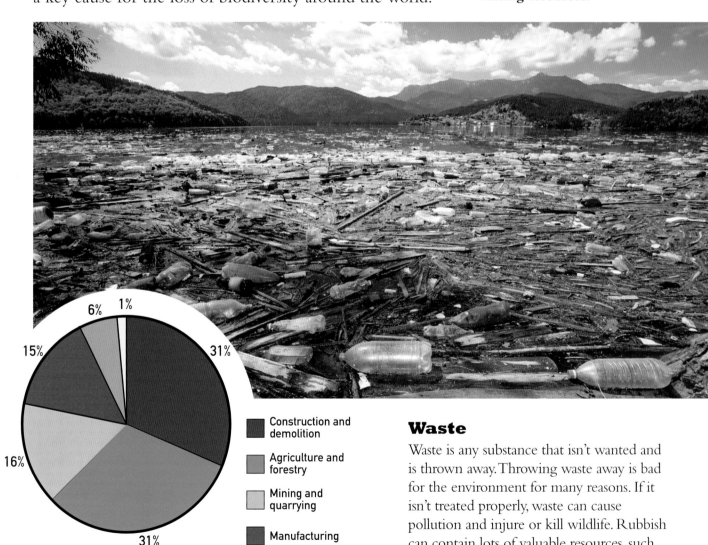

Pie chart percentages: 31%, 6%, 1%, 15%, 16%, 31%

Legend:
- Construction and demolition
- Agriculture and forestry
- Mining and quarrying
- Manufacturing
- Municipal waste
- Energy production

▲ Estimated total annual waste generation in the EU by sector (source: DEFRA 2009).

Waste

Waste is any substance that isn't wanted and is thrown away. Throwing waste away is bad for the environment for many reasons. If it isn't treated properly, waste can cause pollution and injure or kill wildlife. Rubbish can contain lots of valuable resources, such as glass, metal and useful chemicals. If rubbish is just thrown away, these valuable resources are lost.

> 'Pollution kills, poisons, and otherwise impacts the lives of over a billion people, in particular children, every year.'
>
> Blacksmith Institute

▲ People in Pontianak, Indonesia wearing anti-air pollution masks. Pollution affects people's health and reduces their quality of life.

The impact of pollution

A substance is a pollutant if it is present in quantities that cause damage or harm. When large amounts of a toxic substance enter the environment, for example a large oil spill from a supertanker, then it will cause harm. However, even small amounts of pollution can be a problem because levels can build up over time. For example, if plants become contaminated with chemicals and these plants are eaten by an animal, then the chemicals can become concentrated in that animal's body at a dangerous level.

Types of pollution

Pollution is often defined by how it affects the environment. For example, carbon monoxide is a poisonous gas produced by car exhausts. It pollutes the air and is therefore classified as a type of air pollution. Farm chemicals, such as pesticides, can contaminate the soil and river water, and are therefore classed as water and soil pollutants.

Top ten problems

There are a wide range of pollution issues facing the world today. To highlight key problems, the Blacksmith Institute (see page 43) produced the 'Top Ten World's Worst Pollution Problems':

- Artisanal gold mining
- Contaminated surface water
- Indoor air pollution
- Industrial mining activities
- Groundwater contamination
- Metals smelting and processing
- Radioactive waste and uranium mining
- Untreated sewage
- Urban air quality
- Used lead acid battery recycling

Sustainable solutions

Dealing with waste and pollution is a vital part of sustainable development. If these problems are not managed effectively, then the environment will continue to suffer and its long-term survival will be put in jeopardy. This book looks at the main waste and pollution challenges, and highlights some sustainable solutions to the most pressing problems faced by the environment today.

The changing face of pollution

Pollution is not a new problem. Archaeologists have found evidence of rubbish dumps in ancient Rome. However, over time the nature of pollution has changed – as people have moved into large cities and developed new industries, so the scale and character of the pollution challenge has altered. We have also improved our knowledge of which substances are polluting. For example, we now know that cigarette smoke can harm our lungs, but in the 1950s, smoking was advertised as being healthy.

▼ Paddling on a pollution-free lake, USA. Government laws, such as the US Clean Water Act, have helped many regions to combat waste and pollution levels.

Dealing with pollution

The way in which pollution has been dealt with has also changed over time. In the past people got rid of pollution from factories by simply building tall chimneys so that fumes would be carried away on the wind. Sewage was dumped in rivers and out at sea and washed away on the tide to be diluted and dispersed. However, as the amount of pollution that people produced increased such approaches no longer worked effectively and were unsustainable. To try to solve the pollution challenge in a sustainable way, scientists and engineers developed ways to either reduce the amount of pollution produced, capture it so that it did not escape into the environment or treat it so that it became safe.

In more developed countries (MDCs), such as the USA, Japan and the UK, governments have enacted laws to reduce the amount of pollution entering the environment. For example, in the United States, the Clean Air and Clean Water Acts have led to the reduction of smog in cities and the clean-up of many rivers.

Poor performance

While many MDCs have managed to reduce levels of some – but not all – pollution, less developed countries (LDCs) are facing ever worsening pollution problems. The economies of some LDCs are growing rapidly, but many businesses are not investing in technology needed to clean up their factories. This is often because of the extra money it costs and the poorly enforced national laws protecting the environment. In many of these countries, it is often the poorest people, living close to polluting factories or in slums, who suffer from health problems caused by pollution.

▼ **Radiation monitoring in Russia. Monitoring pollution is a vital part of pollution control – it lets us know whether we are controlling pollution effectively.**

Pollution and disease

It is only relatively recently that the link between pollution and disease has been widely understood. One of the most famous breakthroughs took place in 1854 when there was a terrible outbreak of cholera in Soho, London. A physician, John Snow, thought that the problem was caused by polluted water from a well. To prove his point he had the well's pump handle removed and the outbreak of the disease ended.

Silent Spring

One of the most influential books on pollution is *Silent Spring*, which was written in 1962 by a scientist called Rachel Carson. In *Silent Spring*, Carson looked at the impact of pesticides on the environment and highlighted how they were affecting wildlife in the countryside. It is thought that *Silent Spring* helped start the development of new anti-pollution laws that have restricted the use of certain chemicals, including DDT.

'Particulate matter is of great concern. In many Asian cities such as Karachi, New Delhi, Kathmandu, Dacca, Shanghai, Beijing, and Mumbai it exceeds all the limits.'

Liisa Jalkanen, atmospheric environment research chief at the World Meteorological Organisation

A global pollution problem

Many scientists, politicians and environmentalists think that the most important pollution problem facing the planet is climate change. As a result of human activity, a build up of greenhouse gases in the atmosphere is thought by many people to be causing an increase in global temperatures, rising sea levels and other environmental changes which will harm wildlife and people.

The main greenhouse gases:
- Carbon dioxide (CO_2)
- Methane
- Nitrous oxide
- Ozone
- Water vapour
- Halocarbons

Greenhouse reduction

Greenhouse gases are produced by a wide range of activities, but the main ones include burning fossil fuels in power stations, industrial processes, transport, agriculture and the burning of forests.

Many MDCs (which produce the majority of greenhouse gases) have agreed targets to reduce the amount of greenhouse gases they emit. The EU Member States, for example, are committed to reducing greenhouse gas emissions to 8 per cent below 1990 levels by 2012.

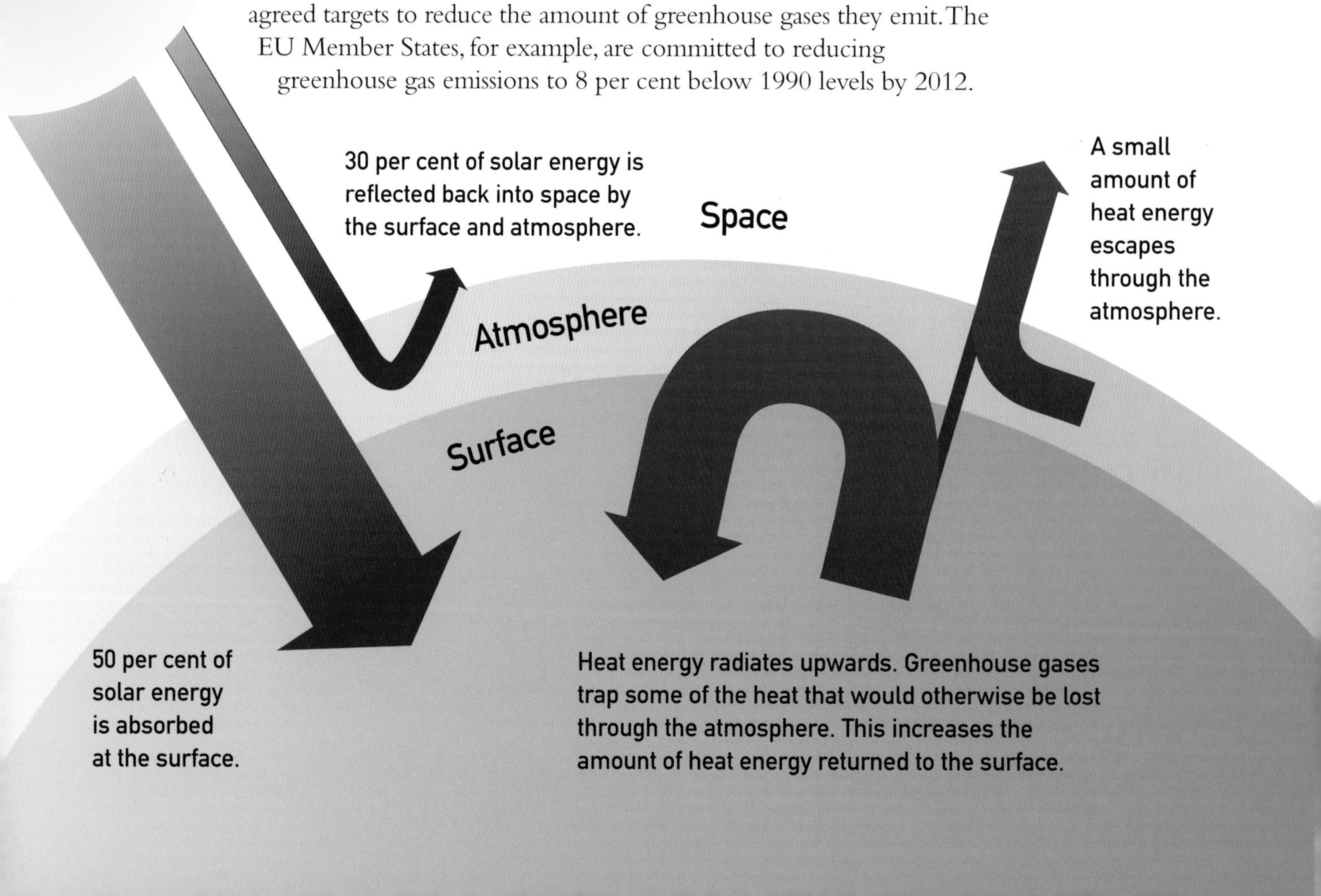

Sun

30 per cent of solar energy is reflected back into space by the surface and atmosphere.

Space

A small amount of heat energy escapes through the atmosphere.

Atmosphere

Surface

50 per cent of solar energy is absorbed at the surface.

Heat energy radiates upwards. Greenhouse gases trap some of the heat that would otherwise be lost through the atmosphere. This increases the amount of heat energy returned to the surface.

▼ The campaign group Greenpeace brings attention to rainforest destruction. The logging and burning of tropical forests creates over 20 per cent of global greenhouse gas emissions.

Campaign pressure

Campaign groups, such as Greenpeace and Friends of the Earth, think that not enough is being done to tackle climate change. They believe that international targets are not sufficient, and are campaigning for tougher action. Now plans are underway to make reduction targets more ambitious in both MDCs and rapidly expanding LDCs.

Making carbon footprints smaller

Almost everyone is responsible for causing some greenhouse gas pollution. Whether it's eating beef (cows produce methane) or turning on a light, many activities are linked to the production of greenhouse gases. The amount of CO_2 an individual,

company – or even nation – is responsible for is called their 'carbon footprint'. In the UK, many things are being done to help companies, organisations, people and places reduce their carbon footprints:

• The UK government has set up the Carbon Emissions Reduction Target (CERT) to force energy supply companies to help people reduce the carbon footprints of their homes. The companies are helping people improve the energy efficiency of their homes by fitting better insulation, and installing heating and lighting that uses less energy.

• The Carbon Trust helps businesses cut down the amount of energy they use. The Trust works with businesses to find ways they can save energy and it

gives out loans to companies that are trying to cut down their CO_2 emissions.

• Environmental groups are helping too. For example, on the WWF website (see address below) people can find out about how to reduce their carbon footprint. WWF have produced a 'footprint calculator' which allows anyone to see how they are doing.

http://footprint.wwf.org.uk

'Measuring your ecological [carbon] footprint takes less than five minutes and could set you on a life-changing journey....' WWF

The throw-away society

Around the world people throw away an incredible amount of waste. This is particularly true for people in MDCs. For example, according to the United States Environmental Protection Agency, in 2007, Americans generated about 230 million tonnes of rubbish. According to the agency, solid waste generation increased from 1.6 to 2 kilograms per person per day between 1980 and 2007.

▲ Thousands of rag-pickers, including adults and children like these, work at dumps in countries such as Bangladesh and Sri Lanka.

Waste challenges in LDCs

In many LDCs, dealing with people's waste presents serious challenges. The collection of waste is often unreliable and ineffective and needs to be improved. What is more, in many poor countries people known as rag-pickers make their livelihoods by scavenging waste piles looking for things they can sell. As waste management is modernised it is important that such people are given a role to play or another way to make a living.

Case study...
The Forgotten Poor

Sri Lanka is a country where the poor have long had a role in dealing with the country's rubbish. In the country's capital city, Colombo, many people work as rag-pickers at the Central Colombo Refuse Dump Yard. This large site is home to a rubbish mountain that stands some 76 metres high and contains toxic waste, including infectious hospital material. The rag-pickers make their living gathering paper, cardboard, tin and other rubbish which they then sell. To help these people, the Department of Social Responsibility of the Methodist Church in Sri Lanka (a partner of Christian Aid) has set up the 'Forgotten Poor' project to improve their health and safety, to help them develop a more sustainable business and to promote recycling. The rag-pickers now have identity cards for the National Programme for Recycling Solid Waste which gives them more rights and helps them make a better living.

Waste challenges in MDCs

In the world's MDCs there has been massive investment in waste management to make sure that rubbish is collected and disposed of safely and effectively. Every year in these countries, hundreds of millions of tonnes of waste are put in specially built giant holes, called landfill sites, and buried. In many countries it is becoming more difficult and expensive to find suitable places to bury rubbish.

Case study...
Burning in Singapore

Singapore is a small island state in Southeast Asia. With a population of over 4.8 million and a highly developed economy, it produces a lot of waste. But being a small island it has a massive challenge disposing of its rubbish. To deal with the problem, most of the waste produced by Singaporeans is incinerated. The ash is then dumped into a specially built landfill 'island' called Pulau Semakau that has been reclaimed from the sea. Pulau Semakau cost hundreds of millions of pounds to build and will be full by about 2040. Because of this, Singaporeans are now being encouraged to reduce the amount of waste they produce and to recycle more. Singapore's waste challenges are a concentrated version of those affecting many other nations.

▼ The large north cell of Pulau Semakau looking across towards the waste receiving station. The whole landfill island has a capacity of 63 million m³.

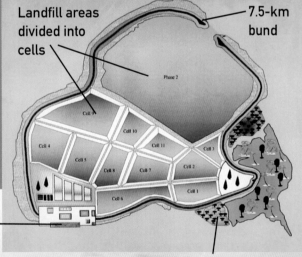

Landfill areas divided into cells

7.5-km bund

◀ A plan of the landfill island Pulau Semakau. The island measures 3.5 km².

Phase 2

Cell 9
Cell 10
Cell 4
Cell 11
Cell 3
Cell 5
Cell 8
Cell 7
Cell 2
Cell 6
Cell 1

Incinerated waste receiving station

Re-planted mangrove trees

Reducing the rubbish mountain

Reducing the amount of waste we throw away is a key environmental challenge. There are many ways in which people, companies and countries can become less wasteful. The most important are called the 3-Rs: reduction, reuse and recycling.

• Reduction: there are many ways to reduce waste, from using cloth nappies rather than disposable nappies, or china plates instead of disposable plates. Products can be designed so that they are durable and use as few raw materials as possible.

• Reuse: refillable milk bottles are an obvious example of reusing something rather than just throwing it away. Refilling empty printer toner cartridges with new ink is another example of reusing something rather than simply binning it.

• Recycling: many products can be recycled. For example, paper can be turned into new paper, glass bottles into new glass and drinks cans back into the metal they were made out of. Many things can be recycled into totally new products. For example, tyres can be used to resurface roads and plastic bottles can be recycled as plastic clothing.

▶ **Steel cans are attracted to an electro-magnet before being processed into recycled steel.**

Focus on recycling: why we should recycle

Every time we throw something away and it isn't recycled we are creating pollution. But we are also wasting the raw materials that the thing we threw away was made from. To make new products we have to mine, grow or otherwise create the raw materials they are made out of. We also have to use energy to transport them – all of which has a massive environmental impact.

According to the Worldwatch Institute, making 1 million tonnes of aluminium cans from virgin raw materials requires 5 million tonnes of bauxite ore and the energy equivalent of 32 million barrels of crude oil. Recycling the aluminium cans, in comparison, saves all of the bauxite and more than 75 per cent of the energy, and avoids about 75 per cent of the pollutants.

Encouraging recycling

Around the world, governments and environmental groups are working to make it easier for people to recycle. For example, many cities and towns now ask residents to separate their recyclables from their waste. The recyclables are then collected in separate containers to be taken away to be turned into something new.

In many US states, recycling is encouraged through the use of a deposit on drinks. Many countries have also brought in laws making it illegal to put certain items in landfill – in the EU, car tyres cannot be thrown away in landfills but must be recycled or otherwise disposed of.

Many other countries have set themselves recycling goals. For example, the UK government's long-term aim is to cut the amount of household waste buried in landfill by 50 per cent per person (from 450 kg per person in 2000 to 225 kg in 2020).

Designing with recycling in mind

To help boost recycling efforts, many companies around the world are designing their products so that they contain more recycled materials. Designers are also ensuring that products are easier to recycle when they come to the end of their useful lives. For example, car maker Renault is designing cars that are 95 per cent recoverable at the end of their lifecycle (recyclable or as a source of energy) and which have at least 5 per cent of their plastic parts made from recycled material.

'Recycling is the best environmental option. It is good for the environment, saves energy, reduces raw material extraction and helps combat climate change.'

Waste and Resources Action Program (WRAP)

▼ Using recycled manufacturing products in the construction industry reduces the need for virgin raw materials.

Reducing food waste

A lot of the rubbish we throw away does not need to be discarded. For example, about a third of the food that people in the UK buy is wasted and thrown in the bin. To get people to use up leftovers and stop food waste, the 'Love Food … Hate Waste' campaign has been set up to show people how to use up all the food they buy. It is run by the UK's Waste and Resources Action Programme (WRAP) that also promotes home composting – another way to reduce food waste. This is just one of the many ways in which people are working to reduce the amount of waste that is produced.

> 'Pollution is nothing but the resources we are not harvesting. We allow them to disperse because we've been ignorant of their value.'
>
> Buckminster Fuller, visionary American architect (1895–1983)

Case study...
Zero waste Taiwan

Taiwan is an island in East Asia just off the coast of China. It has a population of over 23 million people and a modern economy. Dealing with waste from both homes and industry has become an increasingly difficult challenge. To try to address this problem, the country has adopted a 'zero waste' policy that involves a number of steps to not only increase the amount of waste recycled, but reduce the amount of waste produced.

For example, the government has restricted the use of plastic shopping bags and disposable dishes. People are also charged by the bag to have their waste taken away. This encourages them to reduce the amount of waste they produce. What is more, the country's environmental protection agency has made an agreement with convenience stores not to supply disposable chopsticks unless demanded by the customer. This is expected to reduce chopstick use by about 20 per cent, or 36 million pairs, a year.

▼ Shoppers in Taipei City, Taiwan. They are encouraged to reuse bags by restrictions imposed by the government.

Waste exchange

Waste doesn't just come from people's homes. In fact, businesses and industry are responsible for much of the waste that is produced. Waste exchange is one increasingly popular way in which some companies are reducing waste. They are sending their waste to other businesses that can use it as a raw material. For example, many chemical companies produce waste chemicals that can be treated and used again.

▶ Construction waste is separated into different materials so it can be sold on to other businesses.

New buildings from old

One of the biggest waste challenges is created by building and construction waste, which makes up about 40 per cent of the solid waste produced in the USA. Around the world, there are many projects underway to reuse and recycle this waste. In the USA there is a network of hundreds of Building Material Reuse stores, where material from old houses is sold on to be reused. Builders are also taking apart old buildings to reuse and recycle the materials they contain. For example, in Buffalo, a group called Buffalo Reuse revitalises neighbourhoods using reused materials. Through this work, Buffalo Reuse creates community gardens and plants trees that help transform run-down areas into productive green space.

Debate... Is incineration rubbish?

Although waste reduction is vital, there are still massive amounts of waste to be disposed of. Waste incineration is being seen as an important way in which to deal with waste. In many countries, such as Denmark and Sweden, large-scale incinerators use the energy from burning waste to provide heat and generate electricity. For example, about 40 per cent of homes in Malmo (Sweden's third largest city) are heated by a waste-to-energy incineration plant.

Those who oppose waste incineration argue that burning waste produces a lot of harmful gases and ash. They also argue that it discourages people from recycling as much waste as possible. Those who support incineration argue that it significantly reduces the volume of waste that must be sent to landfill and that modern pollution control technology makes incinerators safe.

Do you oppose or support incineration? To what degrees could it be harmful or be helpful?

Polluting power

Whenever you switch on a light, or boil a kettle, you are using electricity. Much of the electricity that we use is produced by power stations which burn fossil fuels, such as gas, oil and coal. Fossil fuels are also used to heat homes and power vehicles and machinery.

'Coal is not only the largest fossil fuel reservoir of carbon dioxide, it is the dirtiest fuel. Coal is polluting the world's oceans and streams with mercury, arsenic and other dangerous chemicals.'

James Hansen, director of NASA's Goddard Institute for Space Studies, 2007

◀ **Environmental group Greenpeace protest as part of their 'Quit Coal' campaign. Coal-fired power stations are being targeted by environmental campaigners as 'fossil-fuelled' dinosaurs.**

Pollution problems

The production and use of fossil fuels causes a lot of potential pollution problems – from the spoil produced by open-cast coal mining to the spillages caused by the transportation of oil. Fossil-fuel power stations produce a range of potentially polluting emissions. These include the gases CO_2, sulphur dioxide (SO_2), nitrogen oxides and particulate matter. Among the pollution problems linked to power generation are acid rain and smog. Acid rain is produced when sulphur and nitrogen oxides react with water; it causes rain to be slightly acidic which can harm trees and other plants and erode buildings.

▼ Coal-fired power stations, like this one near Datong, China, are one of the major sources of poor air quality in rapidly-industrialising nations.

In many countries, laws have been passed to limit the amount of pollution produced by power stations. Steps are also taken to actively reduce the amount of pollution they produce. For example, many power stations use the Flue Gas Desulphurisation (FGD) process which removes SO_2 from waste gases. FGD can remove 95 per cent or more of the SO_2 in the flue gases of a power station. Such technology has helped to tackle the acid rain problem.

Case study··· China's coal challenge

China is one of the world's fastest developing economies. To help drive this growth, the country is rapidly expanding the number of coal-fired power stations it has. Today, it already uses more coal than the United States. Pollution from China's coal use is affecting the health of people in the country and beyond its borders, and is thought to contribute to hundreds of thousands of premature deaths each year. The World Bank has reported that 16 of the world's top 20 most polluted cities are in China, and much of this pollution, including acid rain, is linked to China's coal industry. China is now racing to try to clean up its coal-fired power stations by fitting pollution-reduction technology and pushing the development of cleaner forms of energy.

Debate··· Is nuclear power polluting?

Nuclear power is one of the most contentious environmental issues in the world today. Some people think that the world needs nuclear power. They argue that, in comparison to other types of power generation, it is a 'clean' form of power; it does not produce any significant emissions of the greenhouse gases which are thought to be causing climate change.

Those who do not support nuclear power argue that nuclear power stations are a pollution issue because they produce highly radioactive waste which must be carefully stored for tens of thousands of years. According to Greenpeace, the UK now has enough radioactive waste to fill the Royal Albert Hall in London five times over. Those who oppose nuclear power, also argue that if something were to go wrong at a nuclear power station then the resulting radioactive pollution could be catastrophic.

Which side of the debate are you on?

▼ Graph showing nuclear waste generation from 1985 to 2010 (predicted) in thousand tonnes of spent fuel.

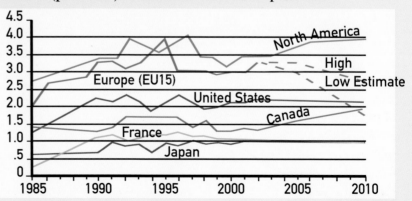

Clean energy

People all over the world are working to find ways of generating power that produces little or no CO_2 or other pollutants.

The clean energy challenge is being met in three main ways:

• First, making conventional power stations less polluting by fitting the latest pollution control technology – see carbon capture and storage (CCS) opposite.

• Second, working to reduce energy demand through energy efficiency. For example, in Japan a campaign called 'Team 6 per cent' encourages people to cut their energy use through a series of actions, such as controlling the temperature settings on air conditioners.

• Third, by producing energy from significantly less-polluting renewable sources, such as wind, water, wave and solar power. For example the European Union has set its member countries a target that around 20 per cent of all energy must be provided from renewable energy sources by 2020.

Tough challenge

The clean energy challenge is a particularly tough one to meet, especially as developing countries such as China and India are rapidly increasing the amount of energy they use. However, many people think that in the future energy generation can be cleaner. For example, according to the environmental group Greenpeace, by 2050, the United States could cut its CO_2 emission levels by over 80 per cent by using energy more efficiently and increasing its renewable energy generating capacity.

▲ Insulating homes effectively reduces energy consumption and waste, and reduces the amount of pollution generated at the power source.

'With the new Obama administration and the new Congress making good on their campaign promises to tackle the global climate crisis, there is new hope that America will once again be a world leader in building a global clean energy economy.'

Greenpeace

Carbon capture

Although renewable technologies provide a way of generating energy in a less polluting way, many people doubt that they will be able to provide a significant amount of the energy that the world needs in the short term. For this reason, a lot of work is being done to see how pollution from conventional power stations can be reduced.

One potential way forward is called 'carbon capture and storage' (CCS). This involves trapping the CO_2 produced by power stations and pumping it deep underground where it is locked up in underground geological formations. This stops it polluting the atmosphere. Although there are only a small number of operational CCS projects around the world, the idea is beginning to take off. In 2009, the British government pledged that no more coal-fired power stations would be built in the country unless some of the CO_2 they would produce is locked away underground using CCS technology.

'We have to make a serious, nationwide commitment to developing new sources of energy.'

Barack Obama, in his campaign to become US President

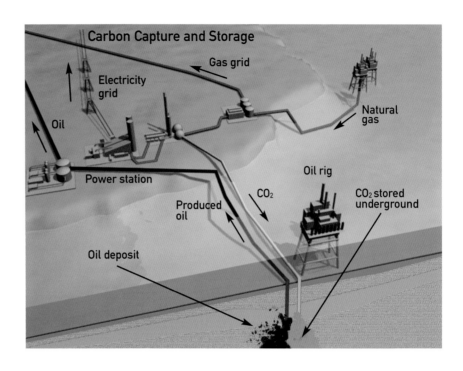

▲ Illustration showing how an existing oil network could be used for carbon capture and storage.

▶ Oil rigs such as this one could be used to pump CO_2 into the earth, as well as extracting oil.

Mirrors in the desert

One of the most ambitious projects to produce energy in a non-polluting way is to use the sunlight that falls on the desert regions of the world to make electricity. This technology, called Concentrating Solar Power (CSP) uses a network of mirrors that focuses the Sun's rays to boil water. This is used to run giant steam turbines and generate electricity. According to the group behind the idea, DESERTEC, by using CSP, less than 1 per cent of the world's deserts could generate as much electricity as the world is now using.

Cleaning up industry

Industrial pollution is any pollution that is caused by industry. Many industrial processes create polluting gases that can enter the atmosphere if the right technology is not used to capture and clean them up. Industrial pollution is also caused when toxic wastes (such as chemical by-products) are not properly treated and are dumped into rivers. Pollution can also happen if industrial raw materials, products or waste are not carefully stored and leak or otherwise get out into the environment.

'The activist is not the man who says the river is dirty. The activist is the man who cleans up the river.'

Ross Perot, American businessman and former presidential candidate

Industrial Revolution

Industrial pollution started to be a major problem in the late 18th century, after the start of the Industrial Revolution. Over time, the problems caused by industrial pollution have led to laws being introduced in many countries that set limits on the amount of pollution a factory can release and which have helped clean up the environment. For example, in the 1970s it was discovered that the health of people at Love Canal (a neighbourhood in New York State) was being affected by thousands of tonnes of toxic industrial waste that had been buried near their homes. This incident helped lead to the establishment of a national 'Superfund' to clean up sites affected by industrial pollution.

▼ Industrial pollution, such as this from factories in China, damages the environment, harms people's health and can ruin their quality of life.

▲ Illegal gold miners in Ghana. They are sieving through the waste (called tailings) of the main mining operation.

Dirty industries

Today, most countries have systems to tackle industrial pollution. However, in some countries, legislation is not adequate or is not well enforced. Also, in many countries, there are abandoned industrial sites that are heavily polluted and need to be cleaned up. For example, in a number of African countries, such as Ghana, gold mining is causing environmental pollution and health hazards; in South American countries, such as Peru, people are suffering from respiratory diseases because of pollution from metal smelting plants; and in Russia, radioactive waste which has not been carefully stored is causing serious health concerns.

Case study... The big clean up

To show the scale of the industrial pollution problem facing people around the world, the Blacksmith Institute has entered into a partnership with the European Commission and the United Nations Industrial Development Organisation to develop a comprehensive inventory of polluted places.

Highlighting the problem of industrial pollution is only the first step on the road to doing something about it. To get the money needed to act, the multi-million dollar Health and Pollution Fund (HPF) was launched in principle in October 2007 by representatives from many countries, the World Bank and other organisations. According to the Blacksmith Institute, which is co-ordinating the HPF, it is hoped that the money will help combat and eventually eliminate toxic pollution in LDCs which has resulted from industrial, mining and military operations. The fund will target over 400 highly polluted locations worldwide that affect more than 100 million people.

Tackling industrial waste

Industrial pollution can be controlled and cleaned up. This can be seen in places such as the River Rhine in Germany. This river used to be heavily polluted by the discharge from the chemical companies that are located along its banks. However, improvements in technology and strict legislation has helped clean the river, which is now home to many plants, fish and other animals.

Zero discharge

Around the world, the most innovative companies are now striving to find ways in which the amount of pollution they produce is reduced at source. One of the approaches they use involves treating a factory's wastes so that they can be used again by the factory; such 'zero-discharge' systems point to a future where factories will produce no pollution at all.

E-waste on the rise

The number of computers and other electronic goods such as mobile phones is growing rapidly. This means that more and more electronic waste (or e-waste) is being thrown away. This waste contains many chemicals that must be carefully disposed of or recycled. If they are not properly dealt with then heavy metals, such as lead, and other toxic compounds, such as dioxins (which can accumulate in animals' bodies and have been linked to diseases such as cancer) can escape into the environment.

▲ **A worker sorts computer parts at an e-waste recycling plant in Guangdong, China. There are about 100,000 people earning their living like this across China.**

Many countries have put in place laws to make sure that electronic products are collected and the raw materials they contain recycled safely. However there is growing evidence that some of this waste is exported to LDCs where it is not properly disposed of. In countries such as Ghana, Africa, and in China, the inadequate disposal of e-waste has been linked to toxic pollution that is affecting the environment and people's health.

Campaign...
Guide to Greener Electronics

To help tackle the problem of e-waste, the environmental group Greenpeace has published a *Guide to Greener Electronics*. This looks at how key electronic firms perform from an environmental point of view. Among the issues that Greenpeace reports on is how companies deal with e-waste and the steps they are taking to remove dangerous chemicals from their products. It is hoped that the report will put pressure on companies to improve their environmental performance.

'E-waste is transported internationally from many countries to destinations where informal recycling and disposal take place, often in small workshops with little or no regulation.'

Greenpeace study on e-waste

Worms to the rescue

In many LDCs, there are significant numbers of industrial pollution waste dumps that need to be cleaned up. Often these dumps are in areas where they affect people's health. One example of the problem was found in Gujarat, India, where, according to the Blacksmith Institute, approximately 60,000 tonnes of industrial waste had been lying untreated for many years and had contaminated the environment and people's drinking water.

An innovative method has been used to clean up the problem. First toxic waste was cleared and sent to a special landfill. Then contaminated soil was treated with worms. As they digested the soil these creatures took in heavy metal contamination which was then concentrated in their bodies, so helping to decontaminate the ground. This project was carried out by the Blacksmith Institute, in partnership with local authorities and non-government organisations (NGOs). According to the Institute, it has been fully successful.

▼ Workers wearing chemical suits remove barrels from a toxic hotspot site in Gujarat, India.

Cleaner consumption

Many of the products we use produce pollution. Pollution and waste are also produced when these things are manufactured and when they are thrown away. However, by carefully choosing the products we use, and using and disposing of them thoughtfully, everyone can play a part in making the world a cleaner place to live.

▲ Replacing traditional light bulbs. Many governments are now working to phase out old-fashioned light bulbs so that everyone uses energy efficient compact fluorescent light bulbs.

Greener alternatives

Almost everywhere you look there are opportunities to reduce pollution. When people change their car they can choose a less polluting alternative; or when they buy a T-shirt, they can choose one made from organic cotton that was not sprayed with chemicals when it was grown.

Governments can also stop pollution by passing laws that make the products people buy less polluting. A number of key pollutants have already been tackled in this way. For example, the Montreal Protocol led to the phasing out of chemicals called CFCs during the 1980s and 90s. These were used as refrigerants and in aerosol cans. The release of CFCs and other similar chemicals into the atmosphere was linked to the destruction of the ozone layer that protects us from harmful radiation from the Sun. Thanks to the ban it is thought that the ozone layer is starting to recover.

Other examples of less polluting products include:

• Phosphate-free washing powder – some washing powders contain phosphates. When these chemicals go down the drain, they can get into rivers and seas and harm the living things that live there. Using phosphate-free products helps stop this pollution.

• Low VOC paints – Volatile Organic Compounds (VOCs) are found in some paints that escape easily into the air and which are linked to a number of health problems such as respiratory disease and skin problems. Using paints that are low-VOC or free from these compounds stops this type of pollution.

• Energy-saving appliances – the less energy something uses, the less pollution it will be responsible for back at the power station. Choosing the most energy efficient product possible is a great way to reduce pollution. To help, there are many labelling schemes in operation. For example, the European Union Energy Label rates appliances such as washing machines, refrigerators and dishwashers from A to G, A being the most energy efficient, G the least efficient.

Debate··· Light bulbs – cradle to grave

Getting a true picture of the amount of pollution a product creates involves looking at every step of a product's manufacture, use and disposal – this is called a 'cradle to grave' analysis.

The importance of this approach is shown over recent concerns about energy-saving compact fluorescent light bulbs (CFLs). These bulbs use about five times less energy and last up to 12 times longer than normal bulbs. They therefore can help reduce pollution from power stations. However, they also contain small amounts of mercury, which is a toxic poison.

So does using CFLs reduce pollution? According to the pressure group Greenpeace, normal 'incandescent' bulbs are probably responsible for more mercury emissions than CFLs as burning coal for electricity emits mercury, and incandescents use much, much more energy. What is more, CFLs can be recycled in ways that stop any mercury pollution being released.

▼ Part of a Greenpeace campaign to phase out traditional light bulbs.

'If all domestic bulbs in the UK were CFLs, then we could cut our CO_2 emissions by over five million tonnes – more than the CO_2 emitted by 26 of the world's lowest emitting countries combined.'

Greenpeace

Indoor air pollution

Inside a house or other building air pollution can be a big problem because it can become trapped and can't be blown away by the wind or dispersed in any other way.

Causes of indoor pollution

Many of the things people do at home or in the places they work – from smoking cigarettes to cooking over an open fire – are significant sources of pollution. Buildings can also be polluted by the things from which they are built, the things that furnish or decorate them, or due to the place they have been built. It is thought that indoor air pollution (IAP) affects many millions of people around the world. Luckily, there are many, relatively easy ways in which it can be tackled and people all over the world are working to address this challenge.

▲ A woman making flat bread on an open fire in El Salvador. Open fires such as this are a major cause of indoor air pollution and a significant health threat in many LDCs.

'Indoor air pollution is responsible for 2.7 per cent of the global burden of disease.'

WHO's World Health Report

Sick Building Syndrome

Sometimes it is not easy to pin-point where pollution is coming from. This is often the case with Sick Building Syndrome (SBS), which causes people in a certain building to feel unwell and, for example, suffer from headaches and fatigue. It is thought that SBS is caused by airborne pollutants such as dust and fungal spores and by chemicals such as ozone from photocopiers or chemicals from cleaning materials. Often the impact of SBS can be lessened simply by opening windows to make the ventilation of a building better and many companies are now acting by, for example, installing filter systems and even putting certain plants in offices to help clean the air.

Radon gas

In certain parts of the world, people are advised to test for a type of IAP which comes from nature. Radon is a radioactive gas that is caused by the natural breakdown of uranium present in rocks and soil. Radon can be found in many places in the United States and other countries. According to the US Environmental Protection Agency (EPA) it is linked to lung cancer and is estimated to cause many thousands of deaths each year.

Testing for radon gas is easy and doesn't cost much money. According to the EPA, the main way to deal with radon is to install a vent pipe system and fan, which pulls radon from beneath the house and vents it to the outside.

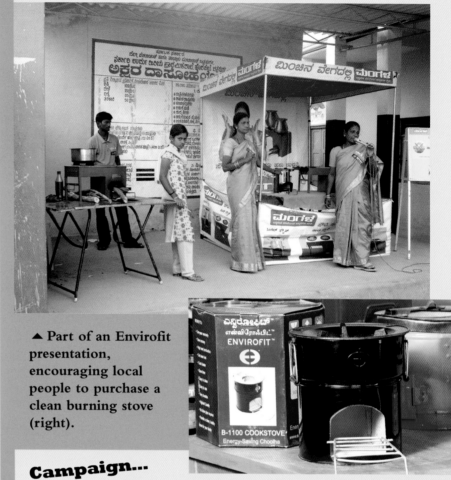

▲ Part of an Envirofit presentation, encouraging local people to purchase a clean burning stove (right).

Campaign...
Clean cookers

It is thought that around half the world's population cooks their food inside their homes using traditional stoves that burn smoky fuels such as wood and dung. The fumes from these fires get into people's lungs and cause a range of respiratory and other diseases. Indoor air pollution of this sort is believed to contribute to the deaths of over a million people a year.

Many of the poor households affected by this problem cannot afford to cook their food using modern electric or gas stoves that cause no IAP. For this reason, many groups around the world are working to find ways in which people can cook their food using traditional fuels without producing dangerous levels of IAP and so endangering their health and that of their families. For example, Independent UK charity the Shell Foundation and leading US environmental nonprofit Envirofit International are working to get 10 million clean-burning stoves sold into developing countries over the next five years. The group has already sold some 15,000 stoves in India alone. These cookstoves are designed to emit significantly less toxic emissions and use less fuel.

Cleaner transport

Transport is also responsible for a large percentage (about 15 per cent) of man-made emissions of greenhouse gases. Because of this, many environmentalists are asking people to choose less polluting ways of travelling – such as bicycles and public transport – and to avoid more polluting ways of travelling – such as cars that have high fuel consumptions, and aeroplanes. In the United States, the Ride Green Campaign aims to get pupils to travel to school in less polluting ways. The Green Education Foundation runs the campaign and is tracking the number of individuals who pledge to 'Ride Green' on the National Green Week website.

'Every time I see an adult on a bicycle, I no longer despair for the future of the human race.'

HG Wells

Technology vs numbers

In recent decades, technological developments, such as lead-free petrol, catalytic converters and improvements in the fuel efficiency of diesel and petrol engines, have reduced the amount of pollution that cars produce. Ultra-efficient motor scooters and hybrid cars that combine conventional and electric motors are among other cleaner technological options that are being developed. However, improvements in technology have been counterbalanced by the increase in the number of cars and other vehicles on the road and transport pollution remains a significant problem.

▼ The Honda Clarity (see opposite) uses a hydrogen fuel cell to power its engine. This technology generates no harmful emissions.

A hydrogen future

The goal for many car manufacturers today is to design cars that produce few or no emissions. One technology that is being developed is the use of fuel cells powered by hydrogen. One pioneering commercial hydrogen-powered vehicle is the four-seater, Honda FCX Clarity. This produces only water vapour as an emission.

The main challenge facing this approach is the fact that hydrogen must be manufactured and that there must be a network of 'hydrogen filling stations' set up to supply the fuel. Producing hydrogen requires energy and, unless this comes from clean or renewable sources (such as wind and solar power), then the production of hydrogen will still be linked to pollution at fossil fuel power stations.

Electric cars, which plug into an electricity supply to get their energy, are another vehicle technology being put forward to solve pollution problems. Many governments, such as those in the USA and the UK, are heavily promoting their development. However, like hydrogen cars, they will only be truly green if the energy they use comes from renewable sources and not from polluting power stations.

▶ **A biofuel production plant in South Dakota, USA.**

Debate...
Is biofuel the answer?

One potential solution to the greenhouse gas challenge is biofuel. Biofuel is made from natural products such as corn, maize and sunflower seeds. Because these crops absorb carbon dioxide as they grow, burning fuels made out of them in a car engine contributes less CO_2 'overall' than using fossil fuels. In some countries, such as Brazil, cars have been running on biofuel for years and many manufacturers, such as Saab, are bringing out cars that run on biofuel.

However many environmentalists oppose biofuels because they think that growing crops for fuel will lead to problems in the supply of food, particularly in LDCs, and will also harm the environment as land is given over to their production.

What do you think about biofuel? Is it an answer to the greenhouse gas challenge?

Pollution on the farm

When farmers use chemicals, such as pesticides and herbicides, on their crops, they can pollute the environment directly and harm insects such as bees and other animals. The chemicals can also be washed from the soil by rain and end up in nearby rivers. This 'run-off' contains chemicals such as phosphorus and nitrogen which can 'enrich' the water in ponds, lakes, rivers and the sea and cause algae to grow. This is called eutrophication. If too much algae grows then it robs the water of oxygen and this can kill many of the plants and animals in the water.

An organic solution

Many countries have passed laws to limit the type and quantities of chemicals that farmers use. However, some farmers have taken steps to phase out artificial chemicals altogether and 'go organic'. Organic farming uses almost no man-made chemicals. Farm animal manure is used as fertiliser and crop rotation is used to keep soil healthy and productive. This approach can reduce pesticide pollution in water and soil and boost the variety and quantity of wildlife present on a farm.

A big gas problem

Farm animals, especially cattle, are big polluters. For example, when they digest their food cows and other animals produce a gas called methane which is thought by many scientists to be contributing to climate change. In fact, livestock is thought to produce more greenhouse gases than all the cars in the world.

▲ The waste gases that cows and other livestock produce could be harming the environment. There are around 1.5 billion cattle in the world.

Case study... Working together to use less chemicals

There are other approaches to reducing the amount of chemicals that farmers put on their fields. For example, the Iowa Soybean Association (ISA) in the USA, which represents 6,000 growers, is working with its members to reduce the over-application of nitrogen fertilisers. Under its On-farm Network, groups of farmers share information from their own on-farm studies and, from that, develop strategies for how and when to apply the least amount of nitrogen for the best economic and environmental results. According to the ISA, growers have reduced nitrogen use by about 30 per cent, or about 30 pounds of nitrogen per acre, without reducing their profit per acre.

'Properly managed, organic farming reduces or eliminates water pollution and helps conserve water and soil on the farm.'

Food and Agriculture Organisation of the United Nations

▲ People like these in Indonesia have been affected by the smoke from burning trees to clear land for farming.

Case study... The Haze

In Indonesia, agriculture and forestry have been responsible for pollution that has affected the health and wellbeing not just of the people in the country itself, but of people living in the nations that surround it. This problem, known as the 'Haze' is caused when vast areas of rainforest, mainly on the islands of Borneo and Sumatra, are burnt to clear the way for farming and plantations.

The smoke from these fires spreads for hundreds of kilometres and has affected countries such as Singapore, Malaysia and the Philippines. The worst Haze was in 1997 and this affected the health and wellbeing of millions of people and cost the region $US4.5 billion. Since then the Haze problem has re-occurred sporadically. Its effect on wildlife has been enormous – vast areas of forest habitat have been lost and many endangered animals, such as orangutans, rhinos and tigers, have been pushed closer to extinction. In response to the problem, a Haze agreement and a Haze fund has been set up by the region's governments. However the problem has still not been solved as farmers and agricultural businesses continue to burn the forest.

Cleaner water

People need un-polluted water to live healthy lives. Polluted water carries diseases and can poison people and animals. Yet, according to the World Health Organisation over one billion people still do not have access to clean drinking water. Water can become polluted in many different ways. Industrial and agricultural spillages and long-term pollution are key problems. Water can also be contaminated by sewage.

Case study... Getting clean water where it is needed

Often the solutions to the clean water challenge are relatively simple. Pumps and wells can help provide uncontaminated water to people who have had to get their water from dirty rivers or streams. Education can also help a lot, by showing people how to make the water they drink safe by, for example, boiling or filtering it.

One example of the kind of innovative work that is being done to provide people with clean water can be found in Africa. Here an organisation

called PlayPumps International has been installing wells that use an ingenious way to pump clean water to the surface. These pumps are powered by roundabouts – children can pump up water as they spin around and play.

According to the group, it has already installed more than 1,200 PlayPump systems in countries such as South Africa, Lesotho, Mozambique, Swaziland, and Zambia, providing the benefits of clean drinking water to millions. The organisation hopes to be able to do the same for many more communities in years to come.

▼ While children play on a roundabout Playpump system, water pumps!

'Around the world millions of children are being born into a silent emergency of simple needs. The growing disparity between the haves and the have-nots in terms of access to basic services is killing around 4,000 children every day and underlies many more of the 10 million child deaths each year. We have to act now to close this gap or the death toll will certainly rise.'

Carol Bellamy, UNICEF's Executive Director

Different places, different problems

Most of the health problems caused by polluted water occur in LDCs, where water is often collected untreated from polluted rivers and streams or delivered though contaminated supply systems. Among the problems linked to polluted water are cholera and diarrhoea, which cause thousands of deaths a day, particularly amongst children. According to the World Health Organisation, 88 per cent of the 4 billion annual cases of diarrhoea are attributed to unsafe water and inadequate sanitation and hygiene.

To do something about this problem, governments around the world have signed up to the Millenium Development Goals and have made a commitment to halve the proportion of the

▲ A woman pumping water in Bangladesh. Changes in water levels have contaminated some sources (see below).

world's population without access to clean water and proper sanitation by 2015.

The arsenic problem

Not all pollution is man-made, and one natural problem that affects drinking water supplies is arsenic poisoning. This problem affects people living in eastern India, neighbouring Bangladesh and other parts of Asia. In many cases, arsenic poisoning has occurred because wells were dug to try to provide villagers with unpolluted supplies of drinking water to replace the surface water they had been using which was giving them diseases. Unfortunately, the

water that the wells produced was contaminated with arsenic from surrounding rocks. If people are exposed to even relatively small amounts of arsenic over time (which is tasteless), it can cause skin problems and even cancer. Work is being done in affected countries to label polluted wells and find alternatives.

Sewage

Today, most cities and towns in MDCs are serviced by complex sewerage systems, and sewage is treated to make it safe. However, dealing with human sewage remains a big challenge. In many parts of the world, sewage is still allowed to flow untreated or only partially treated, into rivers or the sea. This can lead to eutrophication (see page 34) that can kill animals and plants, and cause human disease and even death.

Campaign...
Bag it and bin it

It is not just sewage that goes down the toilet. Each day, people flush a whole range of things away. These include items such as tampons, cotton buds and nappies. Environmental groups such as Surfers Against Sewage (SAS) have campaigned for many years to get people to put these sorts of things in a bag and then dispose of them properly in a bin. According to the Bag It and Bin It Campaign, it is estimated that 2 billion items of sanitary protection are flushed down toilets in the UK every year. This waste can end up in the sea and is washed up on beaches where it can pose a health hazard to surfers and other water users. Animals can also suffer when they try to eat this rubbish or when they get caught up in it.

▶ Sewage treatment works at Wollongong, Australia. Here, sewage is filtered and treated to make sure it is safe, but in many places untreated sewage is still discharged into the sea.

Case study…
Good sanitation and clean water

The link between poor sanitation and unpolluted drinking water is shown in Ethiopia. Ethiopia is an incredibly poor country in Africa and according to the environmental group WaterAid only around 25 per cent of rural and 80 per cent of urban dwellers in the country have access to clean water supplies, while only around 6 per cent of rural and 55 per cent of urban dwellers have access to some form of sanitation facilities. As a result, water related diseases are rife.

To do something about this problem, WaterAid works to provide communities in Ethiopia with good sanitation and water supplies. One successful project that the group has helped put in place is the Robe-Melliyu Gravity Water Supply, Sanitation and Hygiene Promotion scheme. This is situated 430 km south east of Ethiopia's capital, Addis Ababa. Water is in scarce supply in this area and this meant that people did not have enough water to wash with. People were also not used to using latrines and, instead, often defecated in open fields which contaminated water supplies.

Working with the local community and the indigenous NGO Water Action, WaterAid established water supplies sourced from uncontaminated springs. The groups also helped people install hygienic latrines and helped them learn about the importance of good sanitation.

The project has evolved into a community-owned and managed scheme serving a population of at least 70,000. According to WaterAid, everyone now has access to safe water and sanitation coverage is steadily growing.

'Really there was a very big problem before. There was vomiting and diarrhoea. Due to water-borne diseases there were also disease outbreaks. A lot of people died.'

Zeitu Ali, Horeboka village, Ethiopia

▼ NGOs work with local people in many of the poorest regions to build basic sanitation, such as the construction of this latrine in Kenya, Africa.

A cleaner future?

Although great steps have been taken to clean up pollution, there are still many pollution challenges facing countries around the world – from local clean-up problems to the global issue of climate change. Will we be able to solve all of these problems? How will we deal with pollution in the future?

'In the developing world, however, the [toxic pollution] problem is growing because of the drive to industrialise and feed global consumption. Sustainable Globalisation should be a shared responsibility and goal.'

Blacksmith Institute

▲ **Testing new water treatment processes. Future developments in the treatment of waste are being developed in laboratories.**

Taking back waste

Many people around the world already help reduce the environmental impact of their rubbish by recycling. The next step in the development of recycling and waste reduction is known as Extended Producer Responsibility (EPR). This makes it the responsibility of the company that makes a product to take it back from users and recycle it. For example in Saskatchewan, Canada, EPR regulations require the paint industry to manage a consumer take-back program for leftover household paint; while in Europe legislation has been introduced which makes it the responsibility of the producers of electrical and electronic equipment to finance the collection and recycling of waste created by the products they make.

Waste bugs

One of the most cutting-edge ways of dealing with rubbish and pollution is to use micro-organisms to turn waste products into new useful substances. This approach is sometimes called 'upcycling' and there have been successful studies that have used bacteria to turn waste plastic bottles into the raw materials for new higher-value plastics. Scientists have succeeded in genetically modifying bugs so that they eat agricultural waste and produce something that can be used as fuel. Some researchers are even looking at using bacteria to break down plant waste to produce electricity directly.

Large challenges remain

Many MDCs have cleaned up their environment using a combination of effective technology and well-enforced regulations and legislation. However, many LDCs still face the challenge of controlling the pollution that is caused by their development. This is a particular problem in countries such as China and India which are experiencing rapid industrialisation and where the environment remains polluted despite moves by government agencies to try to clean it up.

For example, the River Ganges (also called the Ganga) – India's sacred river – is polluted with chemical wastes and sewage and its waters are so contaminated that, in places, they pose a health risk. This is despite the fact that as far back as 1984, the Indian government launched the Ganga Action Plan to try to clean up the river. Today domestic sewage and industrial discharges, such as raw tannery effluent, are still not treated properly and are discharged into the river. This is because of a failure of legislation and technology investment and implementation. Despite such set backs, many citizen's groups and environmental NGOs have not given up. For example, WWF is working to help restore the river by involving businesses, government and local people. One of its aims is to develop and implement pollution reduction strategies by demonstrating the benefits they can bring to people and the environment.

▲ Water pollution in the River Ganges, India. Many LDCs still face significant challenges that lie in the way of a cleaner future.

Glossary

Archaeologists: people who explore the past by discovering, excavating and understanding the buildings, remains and other artefacts of ancient civilisations.

Arsenic: a poisonous chemical element.

Biodiversity: the variety of plants, animals and other forms of life that exist in a certain place.

Biofuel: a fuel that is made from biological material; often plants which have a high sugar or vegetable oil content. Wood can also be made into a biofuel.

Carbon dioxide (CO_2): a gas that naturally occurs in the Earth's atmosphere. Carbon dioxide is released when fossil fuels, such as coal, oil and gas, are burned.

Carbon footprint: the greenhouse gas emissions caused by an individual, organisation, place, event or product.

Cholera: an infectious disease that can be caught by eating infected food or drinking infected water. Cholera causes diarrhoea – if untreated it can be fatal.

Climate change: long-term, significant change in the world's climate. Many scientists now believe that man-made greenhouse gases, such as carbon dioxide, are responsible for climate change.

Compact fluorescent light bulb: an energy-efficient type of fluorescent light, often designed to replace a traditional type of light bulb.

Contaminate: to make something impure or polluted.

DDT: a pesticide – banned in some countries – that is used to kill mosquitoes and other insects.

Diarrhoea: a medical problem in which people have frequent, liquid bowel movements. It is a leading cause of death in LDCs.

Dioxins: a group of chemicals that are produced in a number of industrial processes and when other chemicals such as chlorine are burned. Dioxins are thought to be a cause of cancer.

Energy efficiency: how much energy a job or task (such as heating or lighting a home) takes to achieve. The more energy efficient something is the less energy it uses.

Eutrophication: an increase in the amount of nutrients in the environment.

Fossil fuels: fuels made from carbon and hydrocarbons, including fuels such as coal, gas and oil.

Global warming: an increase in the average measured temperature of the Earth. Many scientists now believe that man-made greenhouse gases, such as carbon dioxide, are responsible for global warming.

Herbicides: chemicals used by farmers to kill weeds and other unwanted plants.

Hydrogen: a colourless, odourless and flammable gas.

Incineration: a way of dealing with rubbish by burning it in specially designed incinerators which operate at high temperatures.

Less developed countries (LDCs): nations with a low level of economic development.

More developed countries (MDCs): countries that have high levels of economic development.

Ozone layer: a layer in the Earth's atmosphere that absorbs much of the dangerous ultra-violet light that comes from the Sun.

Particulate matter: fine particles of pollution that can be carried in the air and which can cause respiratory diseases and other health problems.

Pesticides: chemicals used by farmers to kill insects and other animals that are pests.

Radon: a naturally occurring gas that is considered to be a health hazard.

Sustainable: something that can continue to take place without causing lasting damage to the environment.

Volatile Organic Compounds (VOCs): gases given off by various chemicals such as paints, glues and cleaners.

Websites

Bag It and Bin It
www.bagandbin.org
The website for the group that is campaigning to stop people flushing the wrong sort of waste down toilets.

Blacksmith Institute
www.blacksmithinstitute.org
Find out more about the Blacksmith Institute and how it is helping to solve pollution problems all around the world.

Christian Aid
www.christianaid.org.uk
Find out more about Christian Aid's work to expose and battle the scandal of poverty.

Friends of the Earth International
www.foei.org
Take a look at the website of the world's largest grassroots environmental network.

Greenpeace
www.greenpeace.org
See what Greenpeace is doing to protect and conserve the environment.

PlayPumps International
www.playpumps.org
Find out more about this innovative organisation, along with campaign news and videos.

Practical Action
www.practicalaction.org
Practical Action believes that the right idea – however small – can change lives. Find out more about its work online.

Surfers Against Sewage
www.sas.org.uk
Catch the latest news from the campaign group that is dedicated to keeping the seas clean for surfers and all other people who love the waves.

United States Environmental Protection Agency
www.epa.gov
Find out more about environmental strategies being implemented in the USA.

WaterAid
www.wateraid.org
Find out what WaterAid is doing to help provide water, sanitation and hygiene education to some of the world's poorest people.

Worldwatch Institute
www.worldwatch.org
The website of the independent research organisation which helps to assist and inform global environmental decision making. Search the 'online features' for more information on sustainability.

WRAP
www.wrap.org.uk
Visit WRAP – the Waste and Resources Action Programme – to find out what businesses can do to reduce the amount of waste they produce and to boost their recycling.

WWF
www.wwf.org
The website of the world-wide conservation group that is working for a future where people live in harmony with nature.

Please note: every effort has been made by the Publishers to ensure that these websites contain no inappropriate or offensive material. However, because of the nature of the Internet, it is impossible to guarantee that the contents of these sites will not be altered. We strongly advise that Internet access is supervised by a responsible adult.

Index

44